Gulbenkian

ARCHITECTURE AND LANDSCAPE

PUBLISHED BY
Calouste Gulbenkian Foundation
Central Services Department

TEXTS
Ana Tostões (Architecture)
Aurora Carapinha, Paula Corte-Real (Landscape)

CONCEPTION OF GARDEN ITINERARIES
Gonçalo Ribeiro Telles

RESEARCH
Aurora Carapinha, Daniela Arnaut, Frederico Fonseca, Gilles Teixeira,
Paula Corte-Real, Tiago Farinha, Tiago Simas Freire

GARDEN ITINERARY MAPS
Filipe Brandão, Inês Chaves

TRANSLATION
Language at Work, Lda.

REVISION
Manuela Vieira Constantino

DESIGN
tvm designers

PRINTING
www.textype.pt

PRINT RUN
1000 copies

ISBN 978-972-98728-7-7
LEGAL DEPOSIT 275 611/08

LISBON, 2012

Calouste Gulbenkian Foundation
Central Services Department
Av. de Berna, 45 A • 1067-001 Lisboa
www.gulbenkian.org

Gulbenkian

ARCHITECTURE AND LANDSCAPE

CALOUSTE
GULBENKIAN
FOUNDATION

50 1956
2006
years

Central Services Department

CONTENTS

Architecture

INTRODUCTION

The Fundação Calouste Gulbenkian Headquarters and Museum is a masterpiece of architecture. The impact it has made and the way it has revealed the power of such qualities as formal austerity and restraint, are proof of the perfect connected achieved between conception and project. Together with its garden, it has forged the prestigious and innovative image of the Foundation itself.

With the objective of showing the public the work and its construction process, the first part of this short book has been organised into seven chapters. The first chapter recalls the presence of Calouste Sarkis Gulbenkian and gives a short history of the site. The second part deals with the process of the incorporation of the Foundation, the choice of the site and the work teams and consultants, before going on to look at the three competition designs entries and studying the winning entry by Alberto Pessoa, Pedro Cid and Ruy d'Athouguia. "From the design to the construction work" is the third chapter, which describes the whole construction process from the project for planning approval submitted in 1961 to the completion of the construction work in 1969. The fourth chapter, "Scales and materials", highlights the importance of the nature of materials and the relationships between architecture and landscape, design and the visual arts. "Beyond the architecture: the Gulbenkian effect" looks at the impact of the Foundation after the complex was opened. Chapter six is dedicated to the CAM (Modern Art Centre), analysing its development, construction and use. Finally, chapter seven, entitled "A gift for the future" looks at the potentials of this architectural complex, highlighting both its value as modern heritage and its capacity to qualify a "green building" by today's standards.

1. THE BEGINNING OF A SUCCESSFUL STORY

Calouste Gulbenkian and his love of art and nature

Throughout his long and intense life, Calouste Sarkis Gulbenkian (1869-1955) amassed an extraordinary collection of art, the large part of which he had gathered since the 1930s in his palace on *avenue* d'Iéna, now the Calouste Gulbenkian Cultural Centre in Paris. In addition to cultivating the arts, Calouste Gulbenkian also nourished a singular love for nature, which was confirmed with the purchase, in 1937, of a property called *Les Enclos* near Béneville-sur-Mer (Calvados) in Normandy, France: "it was merely a huge garden, in which he liked to sit alone, in a good chair, enjoying the enchantment of nature".

His dedication to laying out the park there is testament to the rigour with which he undertook each enterprise and to his interest in the art of garden design. The years of correspondence he maintained with his friend Alexis Léger, a French poet and illustrious diplomat better known by his pseudonym St. John Perse, is also testament to this: "*Les Enclos* is now at an incomparable height of romanticism. The trees I planted have flourished beyond my wildest dreams. [...] The place is enchanting, enveloped in a hemicycle of great planes, around which blue hortensias bloom."

Lisbon – from the Hotel Aviz to Parque Santa Gertrudes

Calouste Sarkis Gulbenkian's sojourn in Lisbon was associated with the Hotel Aviz, a famed luxury hotel located in the heart of Lisbon's Avenidas Novas district. It was there that he set up home in 1942 and lived for 13 years, until his death on 20 July 1955. The day following his death, The Times dedicated two pages to the life of the multi-millionaire and benefactor: under the heading *Great wealth*

Calouste Sarkis Gulbenkian as a child

Silva Graça Palace in 1908. It was to become the Hotel Aviz in 1933

Palace on *avenue* d'Iéna. Now the Calouste Gulbenkian Cultural Centre in Paris

amassed and well spent, it described him as one of the pioneers in the development of the oil business in the Middle East, owner of a vast fortune, and also as a man who had put together one of the most precious art collections in modern times.

Gulbenkian was born in Scutari, Istanbul on 24 March 1869 into a prosperous family of Armenian merchants. He studied at King's College, London, achieving an honours degree from the Department of Engineering and Applied Sciences in 1887. The Times went on to inform the reader that "as an art collector, Gulbenkian is known throught his collection of European painting, which was on loan to National Gallery in London from 1936 to 1950 and was then moved to the National Gallery of Art in Washington, where it is at present on loan. During his many years as an active collector, Gulbenkian has moved from one branch od art to another. His attention has been focused on one thing at time, but he has always been interested in paintings. Gulbenkian is not the typical wealthy collector who is guided interely by experts. Himself a connoisseur, he has of course, had advice in plenty, his various collections bare the stamp of his own individuality and his taste is understandably a reflection of the period in which it was formed. As a philanthropist Gulbenkian has been mainlyconcerned with two things: to avoid publicity as far as possible and to give help to those for whom nobody else catered".

On 31 August 1955, another British newspaper, the Daily Telegraph, reported on the decision of Gulbenkian to offer Lisbon a museum to house his collection.

Dining room in the palace on *avenue d'Iéna*, Paris

Calouste Gulbenkian at Edfu Temple, Egypt. 1930

Les Enclos, Béneville--sur-Mer (Calvados)

Les Enclos, Béneville--sur-Mer (Calvados)

Gulbenkian walking in Les Enclos

Calouste Sarkis Gulbenkian (1869-1955)

The site – Parque Santa Gertrudes

Parque Santa Gertrudes was part of a triangular-shaped property that ended on the southern extreme with a house overlooking Largo de São Sebastião. It was on this triangle traced on the land by the fork created by Estrada de Benfica and Estrada do Rego that first a farm for pleasure was developed – as registered in the map by Duarte José Fava (1833) – and that was later traversed by the new Estrada de Circunvalação (a ring road), as one can observe in Filipe Folque's map of 1857. It was these two pieces of land that José Maria Eugénio de Almeida purchased in 1860, transforming the house into São Sebastião da Pedreira Palace and laying out a park with ponds, a bandstand and nurseries and avenues of exotic trees, where he was also to build stables and coach houses. In 1865, José Maria Eugénio

Duarte José Fava, "Topographic Map of Lisbon and its Suburbs". 1833

Filipe Folque, "Atlas of Topographic Maps of Lisbon", maps nos. 1 and 4. Lisbon, 1857

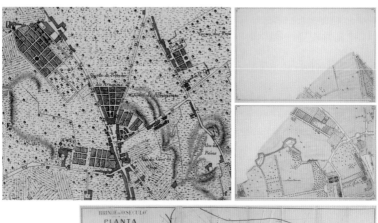

Lisbon Map distributed with the "O Século" newspaper, identifying Parque Santa Gertrudes as the home of the Zoological Garden

commissioned Giuseppe Cinatti (1808-1879) with the construction of a building for stables and coach houses (to be located in the other part of the property, i.e. on the other side of the ring road) that emerge of the vast park designed by Valentim Correia and Cinatti and lovingly cared for by Jacob Weiss, a swiss gardener. This new estate was rechristened by the owner, giving it the name of his mother and daughter: Parque Santa Gertrudes. In 1884 the park became the home of Lisbon's first zoological garden, as one can see in the etchings published in the *Occidente* magazine of that year.

In 1917 a land parcelling plan was drawn up for the park, which, according to the deed, was to be divided into 16 private plots linked by a course laid out in the park, which was to be open to the public on Sundays and holidays. This parcelling project was never carried through and, after housing a horse riding centre and race course, from 1943 the park was used as the venue for the *Feira Popular* fairground, further confirming its vocation as a public space. The greater part of Parque de Santa Gertrudes was sold in 1957 to the Calouste Gulbenkian Foundation for the construction of the Foundation's Headquarters and Museum.

Parcelling project for Parque Santa Gertrudes (1917), consisting of 16 plots linked by a route through the park, which was to remain open to the public on Sundays and holidays

Parque Santa Gertrudes with São Sebastião Palace in the background and the stable building when the park was used as the Zoological Garden (1884)

Aerial view of Parque Santa Gertrudes. 1958

Feira Popular fair on 9 June 1951: "immediately after opening to the public it was overrun at night."

2. PROCEDURE, PROGRAMME AND COMPETITION

The procedure and the programme: 1956-1958

On 18 July 1956 the publication of Decree-Law no. 40 690 legally recognised the Foundation's statutes, thus allowing for the formal incorporation of the Foundation as a worthy way of marking the first anniversary of Gulbenkian's death.

At the same time, the Foundation's Chairman, Azeredo Perdigão, invited the engineer Luís de Guimarães Lobato to help the Foundation in its efforts to find a home. Guimarães Lobato began by creating a work team with the architects Sotto-Mayor and Sommer Ribeiro and the engineer João Hipólito Raposo, which dedicated itself to studying the future premises: it was important to find a space with a public vocation that was capable of receiving a new building and transforming itself into a pole of dynamism in the city of Lisbon. The new construction was to consciously represent the Foundation's image as well as reflect the taste and innermost desire of Calouste Gulbenkian to unite art and nature. After considering the five location options open, the Foundation bought Parque Santa Gertrudes from the Conde de Vilalva on 30 April 1957, as it was considered that "in the location the Foundation building would be fully contextualised by the trees and by the park to the south, which is to be conserved".

At the time in which the competition was being organised, i.e. the late 1950s, the recent British architectural output, in particular the *new towns* (new satellite towns like Stevenage and Roehamp-

Competition programme. An organisational diagram showing the future Calouste Gulbenkian Foundation departments, which was to serve as basis for the architectural design. 1959

Groupings of works of art. Gulbenkian Collection programming files. 1959

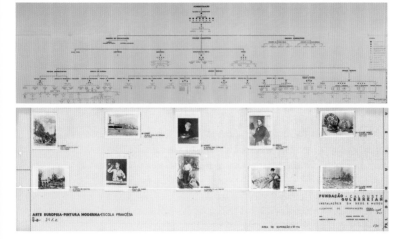

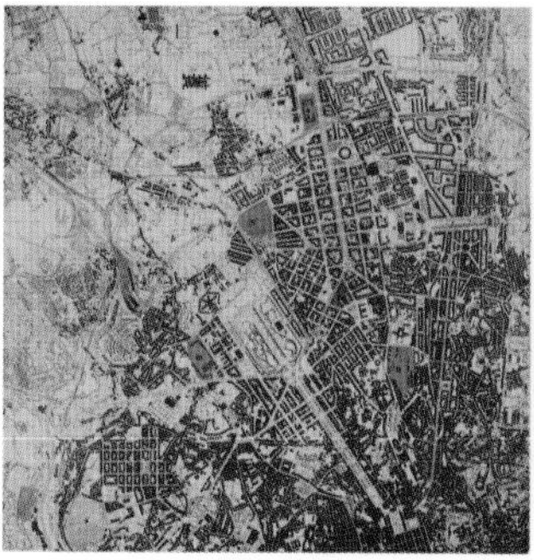

Map of Lisbon identifying the possible locations for the Foundation's Headquarters and Museum in Lisbon. 1956

The Chairman of the Calouste Gulbenkian Foundation, José de Azeredo Perdigão, signing the deed of purchase of the Parque Santa Gertrudes land for the installation of the Foundation's Headquarters and Museum. 30 April 1957

ton) and the Italian experiences in the area of new museum building were some of the dominant references in the universe of architecture. Perhaps for this reason, the Calouste Gulbenkian Foundation had initially considered commissioning a foreign architect, with names like Leslie Martin, J. Dubuisson and G. Lagneau, Franco Albini and Afonso Eduardo Reidy being mentioned.

However, the development of the programme and the decision to create a monitoring team with consultants (both national and international) advised towards holding a competition for Portuguese designers with the objective of "making an important contribution to the advancement of contemporary architecture in Portugal".

The Portuguese architects invited to enter the competition were chosen from the generation born in the second decade of the century and those born in the 1920s, thus constituting a clear investment in the potential modernity of the best Portuguese architecture in the late 1950s.

The competition programme for the construction of the Foundation's Headquarters and Museum drawn up by the SPO (Projects and Works Department) was based on the Gulbenkian Collection programming and the organic structuring planned for the various departments. William Allen and Georges Henri Rivière provided consultancy for the programme, dealing in particular with the building physics and museographic questions, respectively. Leslie Martin, Franco Albini, Carlos Ramos and Keil do Amaral completed the group of consultants responsible for the choice of the final project and the subsequent monitoring of the work.

The defined objective was that the building complex for the Foundation in Santa Gertrudes Park should constitute an important contribution to the advancement of contemporary architecture in Portugal. The Offices, the Museum, the Library and the Auditoriums could have diverse, specific volumes, provided they were capable of constituting a complex of solid architectural structuring in keeping with the importance of the institution and its prominent role in the life of the city.

The Foundation decided for a competition by invitation, inviting three teams to submit their design entries. This solution would guarantee the regular monitoring of the three groups by the national and international consultants, which was indeed carried out throughout the nine months of conduction of studies for the competition (between April 1959 and January 1960).

José de Azeredo Perdigão (Chairman of the Calouste Gulbenkian Foundation)

Luís de Guimarães Lobato (Director of Projects and Works Department)

José Sommer Ribeiro (Projects and Works Department)

Jorge Sotto-Mayor (Projects and Works Department)

Maria Teresa Gomes Ferreira (Museum Curator; Director from 1961 onwards)

Sir John Leslie Martin – Consultant

Francisco Keil do Amaral – Consultant

Carlos Ramos – Consultant

Franco Albini – Consultant

William Allen – Consultant

Georges Henri Rivière – Consultant

The competition and the chosen entry: 1959-1960

The three submitted proposals reflect, with differing senses of radicalism, the crisis of values that was forming in the late 1950s in the context of a period of post-rationalism that had begun to question the International Style and a need for a more humanist, Organic approach. They also revealed the influences of the most diverse trends and revisions within the Modern Movement, such as that manifested in Bruno Zevi's reinterpretation of the spatiality of Frank Lloyd Wright.

Team C Proposal

Frederico George, Manuel Cristóvão Laginha and Arnaldo Araújo.

This design distanced itself from the most canonical architecture of the Modern Movement. Using organic and brutalist references, it was based on the idea of the fragmentation of volumes and spatial complexity.

The complex of buildings was dispersed throughout the park, using an organic construction based on the geometrisation of chamfered squares and octagons that successively adapted to the diverse levels of the land, creating a series of patios.

Preliminary competition design by team C. Implantation Model, view from Av. de Berna and view from the park. May 1960

Team B Proposal

Arménio Losa, Sebastião Formosinho Sanchez and Luís Pádua Ramos.

This solution treated the image of the Foundation as an organism of unusual proportions in an approach that intentionally sought representative monumentality.

The urban identity was assumed by the articulation of three bodies: the office tower; the auditorium and library complex; and, finally, a "special highlight" was given to the circular volume of the museum on the corner of the future Praça de Espanha.

Preliminary competition design by team B. Implantation Model, view from Av. de Berna and view from the park. May 1960

18

Preliminary
competition
design by team A.
Implantation model,
view from Av. de
Berna and views from
the park. May 1960

The right choice

On 20 March 1960, the jury made up of Leslie Martin, Franco Albini, Carlos Chambers Ramos, Francisco Keil do Amaral, Maria José de Mendonça and Luís de Guimarães Lobato, submitted its "Assessment Report on the Three Preliminary Designs for the Construction of the Headquarters and Museum" to the Board of Trustees of the Calouste Gulbenkian Foundation, unanimously suggesting the selection of solution A presented by Alberto Pessoa, Pedro Cid and Ruy d'Athouguia. In the jury's opinion, it was the best study of the three submitted: "it complies with the conditions established in the programme and, in general terms, its design efficiently meets the demands of the departments to be installed in the Foundation's Headquarters and Museum building. We are convinced that the study on the basis of this functional starting point, which has already produced a subtle solution with imagination, can now be taken even further".

The Headquarters, Museum and Auditorium complex emerged as a whole, in which the departments interpenetrated each other nat-

Photo montage

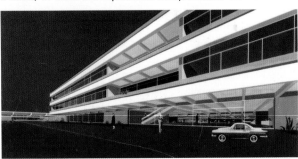

urally and the public could circulate with fluidity. It did not have rigidly demarcated sectors so as to achieve an ambience of a cultural arts centre through the creation of a certain continuity of spaces that acknowledged the concurrent presence of the Foundation's various activities. That ambience was very much enhanced by the integration of the buildings into the park.

Although the design submitted to competition was signed only by the invited architects – Alberto Pessoa, Pedro Cid and Ruy d'Athouguia –, the truth is that the cooperation of the landscape architect António Facco Viana Barreto in the initial phase constituted a basis for the main options in the solution. Indeed, the know-how that Viana Barreto had acquired while designing the green terraces for the Hotel Ritz in Lisbon was extremely important as it allowed him to amplify the conception of the green plane to a larger scale, working with the ambiguity between gardened terrace and garden in the real sense.

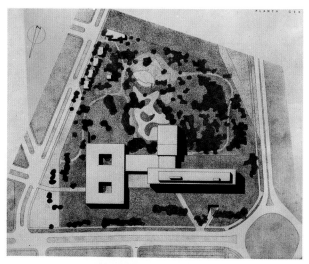

Preliminary competition design. General plan. May 1960

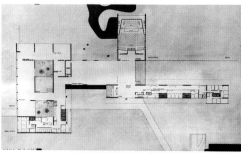

Preliminary competition design. Entrance level plan. May 1960

Preliminary competition design. Transversal sections of Headquarters, Auditorium and Parking lot. May 1960

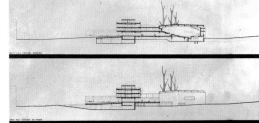

Preliminary competition design. North and west elevations. May 1960

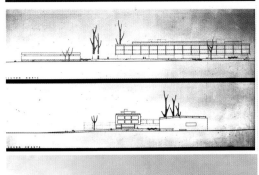

Preliminary competition design. Transversal sections of Museum. May 1960

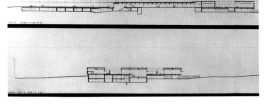

Preliminary competition design. South and east elevations. May 1960

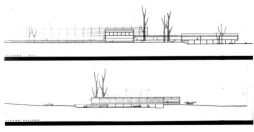

**Alberto Pessoa
Pedro Cid
Ruy d'Athouguia**

3. FROM THE DESIGN TO THE CONSTRUCTION WORK

The Project for Planning Approval

The project for planning approval was submitted on 31 July 1961 with a descriptive memoir that stated that the architectural design of the Foundation's Headquarters and Museum complex was the result of compliance with the conditions in the programme and attentive interpretation of the humanist orientation and predominantly cultural character of the institution, together with the aim of integrating the complex into the natural surroundings of the park in homage to the contemplative spirit of the Foundation's founder: "The current topographic conditions of the site, where the larger trees are located in an area that is more elevated than the whole northern rim of the plot, made it possible to install a huge underground floor in the already existing depres-

Project for Planning Approval. Model. View from Av. de Berna. 1961

Project for Planning Approval. Model. Aerial view. 1961

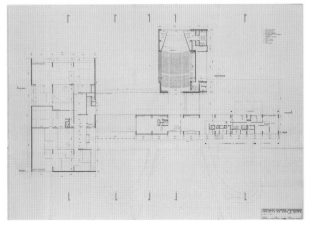

Project for Planning Approval. Entry level plan, Headquarters. 1961

22

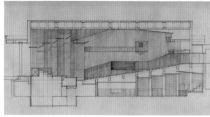

Study for the Headquarters entrance

Study for the Headquarters entrance foyer

Study of the Auditorium interior. Longitudinal section. 1961

Hall of the Auditorium and the Temporary Exhibition Gallery

Auditorium. South elevation. 1961

Study for the Museum body. View from entrance

Study for the Auditorium body. View from the garden

Study for the Museum body seen from the garden, with the library entrance at ground level.

sion, whose covering creates a gentle artificial elevation that perspectively accentuates and enhances the whole architectural composition. The distribution of the construction volumes fundamentally followed a desire for horizontality, allowing one to read the continuity of the green space beyond the constructions and in all directions".

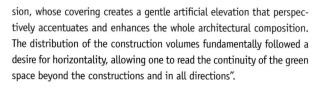
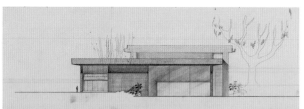
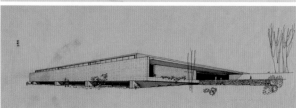

The Headquarters

Of the three structures in the complex, the Headquarters building, located in the north of the park is the one which most stands out.

This sober, rational, and markedly horizontal structure is distinctive for its laminar exterior, its modular repetition, austere design and the hard quality of the materials which shape it, concrete and glass. Located on a higher elevation than Avenida de Berna, precisely on the same level as the enormous eucalyptus that the architects decided to keep, it uses the covering of the underground car park to give form to a suave gardened acropolis that monumentalises the building. In the internal spaces, it comes closer to the human scale with its comfortable, luminous and low-ceilinged atriums that are gently linked by stairs seeking relations of surprise with the garden. The body of the Headquarters building thus achieves an intelligent symbiosis between the desired representativeness and the human values of a modern and civilised space.

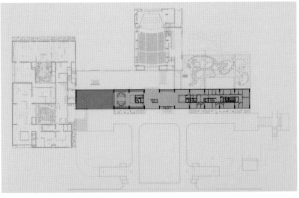

Gulbenkian Headquarters and Museum. Plan with the Headquarters body

Headquarters
■ Served spaces
■ Serving space

Foyer of the Auditorium and access to the congress area. Interior perspective

Foyer of the Auditorium. Interior perspective

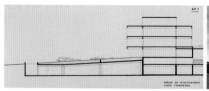

Headquarters
and Parking lot.
Transversal section

Headquarters. 1969

Headquarters.
Interior patio in the
congress area. 1969

Headquarters and the
Auditorium. Entrance
foyer 1969

Headquarters.
Concrete slab roof
over the congress
area. 1967

Gulbenkian
Headquarters and
Museum. Parking
lot plan.

Gulbenkian
Headquarters and
Museum. Plan with
Temporary Exhibition
Gallery

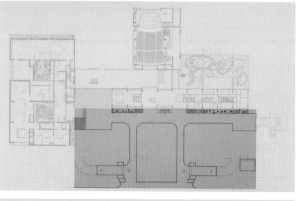

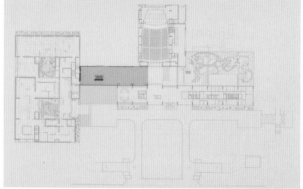

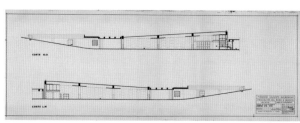

Parking lot. Sections – entry and exit ramps. 1965

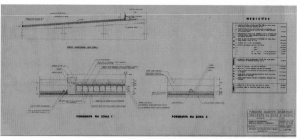

Parking lot. Roof details. 1965

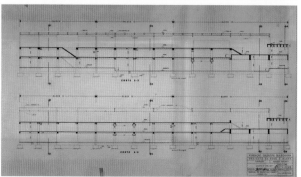

Temporary Exhibition Gallery. Longitudinal sections. 1963

Parking lot. 1964

Parking lot. 1969

Temporary Exhibition Gallery. 1967

Temporary Exhibition Gallery. 1969

Gulbenkian Museum

The Fundação Calouste Gulbenkian Museum is located to the east of the garden and has a separate entrance from the Headquarters building. The project developed so quickly and determinately from the time of the competition proposal up until planning approval, that by 1962 the major decisions had been made. From the initial sketches with brash large window panes which envisioned a two-story building, it evolved into a more rational and restrained form, a horizontal unit in harmony with the garden, which at the same time negated the rhetorical and historic image of a museum. It was endowed with a noble character being the only building to have a stone-lined exterior. Seeking a balance between artificial and natural light, the initial solution settled on an overhead lighting system which was later abandoned and replaced by one which was more controlled in terms of its openings and its relationships between the interior and exterior in order to fit it in the landscape between the patios and the garden. The new bays design was defined to harmo-

Gulbenkian
Headquarters and
Museum. Plan with
the Museum

Gulbenkian Museum
▨ Served space
▧ Serving spaces
▩ Serving space

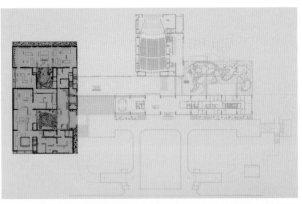

Museum. South
elevation. 1966

Longitudinal section.
1963

Museum. Level 3
plan. 1962

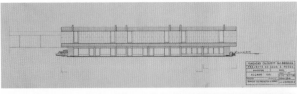

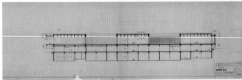

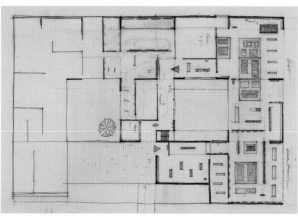

Museum. Distribution of art works

nize with the modular format of the structure. The main matrix-like structure had long units and was spatially austere, linking public and private spaces while at the same time delineating the two inner patios of the Museum.

This project was based on reflecting the essence of the programme, the exceptional qualification of the construction, the intimate relationship with the green space, revealing the symbiosis achieved between the design and the project – whereby the design is understood as the formulation of the basic idea and the project as moving from the design to the construction work.

Museum. Studies

Museum. 1969

Aerial view of the Museum roof, showing the beams that define the space and the enclosed patios

Museum. 1966

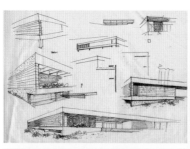

Auditorium

The Auditorium is located south of the Headquarters and temporary exhibit buildings. It is the most inner structure of the complex, situated in the center of the park and protected from surrounding noise.

In formal terms, the compact structure of the Auditorium reflects the rationality envisioned for the entire complex and establishes a real and direct relationship with the acoustics to which it was subject. This is demonstrated by the broken turtle's shell-shaped covering, which the consultant Keil do Amaral suggested as a compromise solution to decrease the size of the exterior structure and yet comply with the need for the increased ceiling height initially imagined and the aim to maintain greatest possible horizontality.

In functional terms, the choice of using an inverted "web" on the stage, made up a system of elevatory platforms combined with a set of spinning walls and a hanging "canopy" over the stage, represents a concept aimed primarily for musical performances but versatile enough to be "tuned" in order to make conference presentations, movies and ballet and modern theater performances possible.

The upright surfaces of the Auditorium are entirely covered in strips of mussubi wood to satisfy different acoustic requirements. The auditorium floor is carpeted and the ceiling is lined in bronze and incorporates the lighting and air-conditioning features. The double glass wall at the back of the stage makes is possible to display the natural scenery open to the south over the pond, and the direct relationship between the indoor auditorium and the park and open-air amphitheater.

Gulbenkian Headquarters and Museum. Plan with the Auditorium

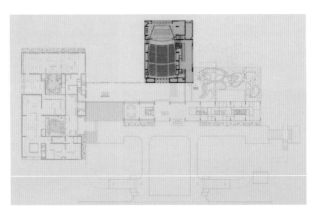

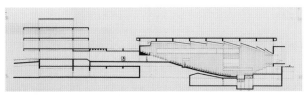

Auditorium and
Headquarters.
Longitudinal section.
1960

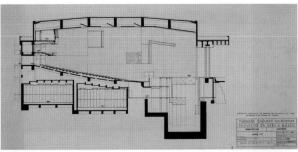

Auditorium.
Longitudinal section.
1967

Installation of
the glass in the
Auditorium. 1968

Construction of the
Auditorium. 1966

Auditorium. 1969

Auditorium. Interior.
1969

4. SCALES AND MATERIALS

Materials

The simplicity and austerity revealed in the choice of materials strengthened the work's restrained and somber qualities. Only three materials were used on the exterior: a poured concrete structure with "visible" finishings; the stone, granite, was used exclusively on the upright surfaces of the Museum building thus ennobling it and differentiating it from the Auditorium and Headquarters buildings; finally, bronzed glass with oxidized brass frames are used on the largest construction surface, causing the glass plane to recede and strengthening the shadow effect and the absence of material. The same care was taken in the choice of woods inside, from mussibe to ash, and on the floors, from hard stone to the comfort of carpeting.

Face concrete

Granite

Window frames
(bronze glass,
oxidised brass)

Mussibi wood

Ash wood

Carpet

Headquarters. 2005

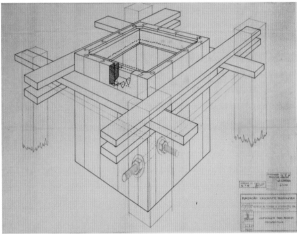

Glass panels in the
Grand Auditorium
supplied by the
German firm Glasbau.
1968

First prototype of
the *Crittall* windows.
1966

Detail of the face
reinforced concrete
structure. 1966

Formwork for pillars
revealing the tongue
and groove joints.
Perspective. 1964

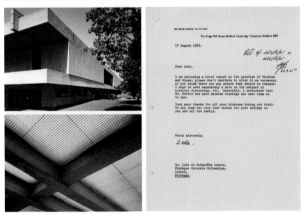

Museum. Structure
in face concrete and
external covering in
granite. 1969

Headquarters. Detail
of reinforced face
concrete beam and
false ceiling with
strips of pinewood

Report by Sir Leslie
Martin to Luís de
Guimarães Lobato
advocating the use of
Crittall frames. 1965

Incorporating the arts

The architectural space was completed with interventions commissioned from portuguese artists from three generations, of which one can highlight: Almada Negreiros and Jorge Barradas representing artists who emerged in the second decade of the century; João Abel Manta representing those who became known in the 1950s; and Artur Rosa, Manuela Jorge and Vítor Fortes representing the youngest generation.

Almada Negreiros opens the space of the entrance foyer with his *Começar* (Beginning) panel, which synthesises his exploration of the "number" throughout his whole life. It is a complex graphic composition in stone measuring 12.90 metres by 2.20 metres, on which Almada carved a quotation from Alain: *Kant m'appri qu'il n'y a point de nombres et qu'il faut faire les nombres chaque fois qu'il faut les penser.*

Further along, on the other side of the wall in the space that connects the entrance to the Auditorium to the lower congress level, Artur Rosa crosses the limits of the interior space with a sculpture in flowing movement that dematerialises spheres, planes and cubes (made of steel, aluminium and acrylic glass) that are projected in the exterior.

For the café and social rooms on the last floor of the Headquarters building, Jorge Barradas created two powerfully figurative and vividly coloured ceramic panels. In the access area to the Auditorium, Victor Fortes conceived a bas-relief in clear polymer as an abstract etching in relief.

João Abel Manta designed a tapestry pattern full of movement and colour that covers the wall with its textile suaveness and contributes to the unusual modernity of the magnificent Sala de Honra.

Cafeteria, with the polychromatic ceramic panel by Jorge Barradas in the background

"Começar" panel. Almada Negreiros. Study. 1969

"Começar" panel. Almada Negreiros. Foyer, Headquarters of the Calouste Gulbenkian Foundation. 1969

Sculpture by Artur Rosa. Model

Sculpture by Artur Rosa

Tapestry by Manuela Jorge. 1969

Museum café. 1969

Panel by Vítor Fortes in the café next to the Auditorium. 1969

Tapestry by João Abel Manta in the Sala de Honra

Interior design

The Foundation complex was the first construction project in Portugal in which it was possible to approach the interior design with professionalism on a grand scale. A sign of the growing recognition of design as an emerging discipline in the 1960s, the application of the global design concept was transformed into a fact of civilisation, contributing to creating the Gulbenkian image of prestige – excellence, sobriety and essentiality.

For Daciano da Costa, decoration gave way to the concept of interior design, which incorporated an approach based on systems of modules subjected to a metric rule, to a regulating guideline. In the interior spaces he work on (the library, café and respective foyer; the Auditorium café; the café) and in the furniture he designed, he regarded the design as an extension of the architecture. With the ingeniousness that characterised his work, Eduardo Anahory designed the Sala de Honra and the Auditorium. Rogério Ribeiro and the designer Victor Manaças assisted the architect Sommer Ribeiro, who coordinated the conception of the museum structures.

The Museum in itself constitutes an unprecedented programmatic and spatial approach, in that the type of the works of art suggested the various solutions found. As the curator, Maria Teresa Gomes Ferreira, put it: "all the solutions in terms of museography were debated at length, namely: the dimensioning of the spaces; the linking of sections; the distribution of the works of art; studies on the showcases, plinths and other supports; studies on diverse covering materials; the appropriate lighting in each given case; and the correct climatology. The integration of the Museum into the park, allowing for moments of reflection and contact with the exterior, the enhancement of the works of art without impositions by the 'architecture', thus favouring the neutrality of the space placed in the service of the collection".

**Reading chair.
Daciano da Costa.
1968**

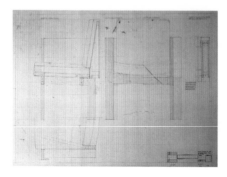

European Painting

Museum. Islamic East

Sala de Honra.

Seats and tables

Administration room.
Sitting area

Library.
Main vestibule

The garden and protected area

The landscape architects Gonçalo Ribeiro Telles and António Facco Viana Barreto officially began work on the project for the park in May 1961. In July of the same year they submitted their first sketch, a synthesised version of which was included in the general plan submitted for building permit application.

One should point out the importance that the Foundation attached from the very beginning to the question of the creation of a protection zone. The process was formally begun in April 1961 through a letter to the Minister of Public Works requesting the establishment of such a zone with a view to safeguarding the architectural complex to be erected in Parque Santa Gertrudes.

Preliminary landscape architecture design. Modelling of the land. 1961

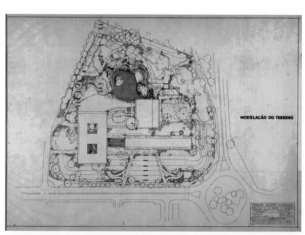

Preliminary landscape architecture design. Circulation routes. 1961

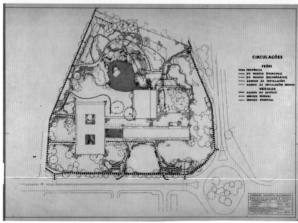

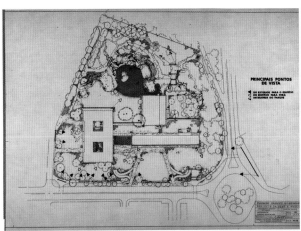

Preliminary landscape
architecture design.
Main viewpoints.
1961

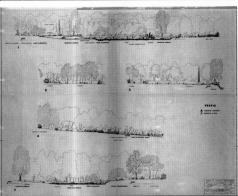

Preliminary landscape
architecture design.
Profiles. 1962

Protection zone. Plan.
1962

Information on the
protection zone.
1961

Garden. 2005

Construction of the
pond. 1963.

Construction of the
pond. 1963.

38

5. BEYOND THE ARCHITECTURE:
THE GULBENKIAN EFFECT

A work of international dimension, designed in the late 1950s and built throughout the 1960s, the Gulbenkian Foundation was a ground-breaking example of what was to happen in other urban centres in Western culture: a cultural arts centre as a dynamising pole of collective life. The architecture was the embodiment of the image of the Foundation, revolutionising the panorama and the meaning of a cultural space in Portugal. The Headquarters, Museum and Garden complex represented a new and contemporary monumentality that, at the time, was very much unique, even at the international level.

In the national context, it reflected the maturity and competence of Portuguese architecture and the opening to the future in a situation of contemporaneity that was hitherto unknown in Portugal. In 1970 the building was greeted as an affirmation of life in the multitude of its cultural functions both in Lisbon and in the country.

Aerial view. 1969

Arquitectura,
3rd series, no. 111.
September - October
1969

Valmor Prize.
Diploma. 1975

Travelling Libraries,
created in May
1958

The Travelling
Library scheme
began working
with fifteen units
for sixty-eight
municipalities

Inauguration
of the Calouste
Gulbenkian
Foundation
Headquarters and
Museum Building.
2/3 October 1969

Inauguration
programme for
the Calouste
Gulbenkian
Foundation
Headquarters and
Museum Building.
Cover. 1969

Visit by Maria
Helena Vieira
da Silva to the
Foundation on
the occasion of
the exhibition
of her work in
the Temporary
Exhibition Gallery.
1970

Maria Helena Vieira
da Silva exhibition
at the Foundation.
27 July 1970

Auguste Rodin
exhibition (80,000
visitors). 1973

6. THE CAM – INFORMALITY AND FLEXIBILITY: 1977-1983

A decade after the opening of the Gulbenkian Headquarters and Museum, the idea emerged to create, within the Foundation, a cultural arts centre that placed the emphasis on a more informal fruition of art that would attract different audiences.

The Centre Pompidou phenomenon (1979), the young Portuguese democracy (1974) and, generally speaking, the changes brought about since "May 1968" in habits and mentalities favoured the expansion of the Gulbenkian Foundation's cultural activities in a multidisciplinary direction, strengthening the internationalisation and cosmopolitism aspect. In addition to this, one should add that, in the course of its support to the visual arts, the Foundation had since amassed a valuable collection. It had purchased works from its scholarship students and the collections of other artists (including works of Amadeu, Almada, the Delaunays and Maria Helena Vieira da Silva/Arpad Szenes) and regularly showed these works in travelling art exhibitions throughout the country. Furthermore, the lack of a museum dedicated to modern art in Portugal reinforced the desire to give the collection a worthy home.

Portrait of Fernando Pessoa. Almada Negreiros 1954

Entrada (Entrance). Amadeu de Souza Cardoso. 1917

To this end, in 1977 the Foundation's Chairman, José de Azeredo Perdigão asked the architect Sommer Ribeiro (Director of the Exhibitions and Museography Department) to conduct a study on the possible location and surface area required for the construction of the CAM (Modern Art Centre), which would establish a natural link with the Headquarters and the Museum and the open-air theatre and also on the possibility of establishing an Open-air Sculpture Museum. With its essentially pedagogical and cultural educational objectives and equipped with a centre for research and divulgation of the various fields of modern art, it was determined in 1979 that the CAM would

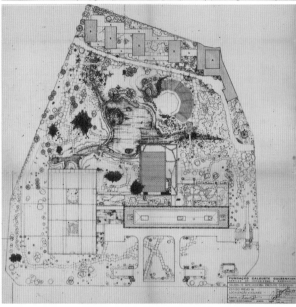

have as its basis the permanent exhibition of the art works already owned by the Foundation.

The idea of organising other events accentuated the multipurpose character of the space, which was to include spaces for cultural education (for events such as meetings of artists, debates, audiovisual shows, performances, etc.), for modern art documentation and archive services and for experimental studios. Once the programme was defined, the design of the CAM was commissioned from the English architect, Sir Leslie Martin, who had been a consultant to the Gulbenkian Foundation for many years.

Articulating two separate bodies – a Museum of Modern Art and an Arts Education Centre – which were to be linked by a common area made up of the reception foyer, the sales area and other spaces of support to the visitor such as the café, Leslie Martin developed the

Diagram of the main spaces

Hypothesis 1 for implantation of the building. Built solution

Hypothesis 2 for implantation of the building. Solution in which the building backs on to the southern boundary of the garden

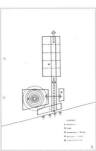

Hypothesis 3 for implantation of the building. Pavilion-based solution

Circulation diagram. Entrance and Main exhibition nave

Circulation diagram. Entrance and Main exhibition nave

View from the garden. Model

Aerial view. Model

Building in construction. 1981

Main exhibition nave. Perspective

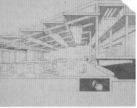

Main exhibition nave, upper and lower level. Structures project. Transversal section 4-4

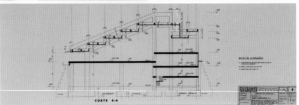

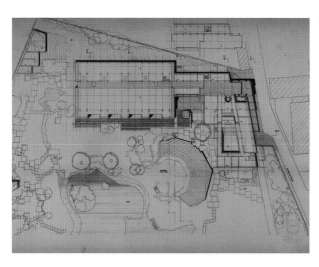

idea of a container building in which the various parts are contained within one single volume: the main exhibition nave.

In contrast to the preliminary design by Sommer Ribeiro, which was based on small pavilions dispersed in the garden, and more fluid implantation solutions, the option for the container building ended up closing the garden. This closure of the green space, which was now confined between two constructions, broke the original axis of the site – Santa Gertrudes Parque – from its original trapezoidal form.

The building was organised in an L shape, with the main exhibition nave serving as a base: a long body, in which the large volume is scaled down by successive horizontal planes complete with hanging plants. Backing on to the southern limit of the garden, the nave articulates in the perpendicular with the body of the entrance foyer that dominates the urban front to the west.

An underground tunnel connects the CAM to the Open-air Amphitheatre, the workshops and the Headquarters and Museum underground car park, reasserting the unity of the Gulbenkian building complex.

The large nave of the permanent exhibitions, with a surface area of some 1,600 m², is extended over three interlinked spaces: the main level, which houses the Portuguese painting and sculpture collection; the upper level, dedicated to foreign painting and sculpture; and the lower level, where drawings, etchings, books and other multiples are exhibited.

The completely flexible exhibition space, which combines natural and artificial lighting, was achieved by means of a structure (designed

Main exhibition nave.
Pinturas para o Céu
Exhibition.
The CAM supported
the encounter
between artists and
the public through
its architecture based
on flexibility and
versatility of the
space

by the engineer Sena da Fonseca) consisting of a series of porticos
with two inclined cross beams spanning 20 metres. The remaining
areas of the museum contain the administrative offices and the storage rooms. The latter are of capital importance in a museum in constant evolution.

Storage

**Main exhibition nave.
Upper level**

Main exhibition nave

Multipurpose hall

7. A GIFT FOR THE FUTURE

From the idea of modern heritage to the concept of the healthy building

The complex of the Gulbenkian Headquarters-Museum-CAM buildings and Garden was the first architectural composition of the 20th century to be distinguished with classification as a national monument. This distinction confirmed the care that the Foundation has had in maintaining the buildings and looking after the garden.

Gulbenkian Museum. European Painting. Intervention by Paul Vanderbotermet. 1999

Gulbenkian Museum. Islamic East. Intervention by Paul Vanderbotermet. 1999

Art Library. Intervention by Daciano da Costa. 1994

Archives. Intervention by Teresa Nunes da Ponte. 2006

Conserving the modern, which is simultaneously something of a cliché and a spectre in architectural restoration, does not mean "reproducing the modern". Today, after almost thirty-seven years of use, the Headquarters and Museum building has been able to adapt to the needs in terms of space and use. Without altering the building's essential values, the interventions carried out focused above all on the renovation of the Museum (a Paul Vanderbotermet project) and the entrance foyer, with the installation of a book shop in the temporary exhibition gallery (a project by Daciano da Costa and Headquarters floors (by Jorge Spencer).

The recent interventions in the congress area, with the transformation of the smaller Auditoriums Two and Three, have confirmed the effectiveness of more thorough remodellings, which, thanks to

CAM. Entrance

Auditorium 2.
Intervention by
Teresa Nunes da
Ponte. 2005

Dressing room
corridor .
Intervention by
Teresa Nunes da
Ponte. 2004

Book shop.
Intervention by
Daciano da Costa.
2000

Auditorium 3.
Intervention by
Teresa Nunes da
Ponte. 2006

Auditorium 3.
Intervention by
Teresa Nunes da
Ponte. 2006

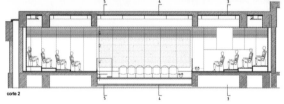

the faithful interpretation of the "original value", resulted in qualified enhancement of the spaces. The design project by Teresa Nunes da Ponte, which re-interpreted the original spatial concept in its relationships of scale and articulation between the interior and the exterior (the garden), responded adeptly to the current usage needs, reinstating with care and attention essential elements of the initial design which, had since been modified (thanks to meticulous research in the archived documents).

Today, it is unanimously recognised that carrying out interventions in modern heritage means linking conservation with documentation. For this reason, the examination and study of the existing structures, in combination with maintenance and processing of the archived documents, proves to be a fundamental task for guaranteeing the quality and effectiveness of the transformations. For the future only makes sense if it incorporates the values of the past.

If the transforming action prerequires working with memory, that of adapting prerequires an ability to respond to the current standards of comfort of the built environment.

At the beginning of the 21st century, the will to guarantee principles of sustainability, with a reduction in energy consumption, has orientated the aim of achieving effective environmental comfort in the Gulbenkian Headquarters and Museum building. The quality of the building, reflecting the paradigms of excellence that have accompanied the process from the beginning – from the project to the design and to the construction work –, and which was based on the most demanding building physics standards, has proved to be the guarantee of that capacity of resistance to time and use.

Today, the desire to declare the building "healthy" has required diverse actions, such as: adapting the ventilation levels and air conditioning levels; adapting materials used in the light of current standards; revising the ways in which the closed spaces are used; harmonising the insulation and eliminating noise; harmonising the relationship between the built interior and the garden exterior. Maintaining and monitoring these systems with a view to achieving a "healthy building" has meant that certain no longer recommendable materials and substances have had to be removed to guarantee quality environmental conditions. Also, as part of the overall process known as performance assessment, the qualification of the building as a "smoke-free building" is one more guarantee of classification as a "healthy building".

Shaping this new era will also include the desire to open the Foundation to new audiences and new geographic regions, redimensioning spaces and uses. It is with this contemporaneity in mind, encompassing the values ranging from the "modern heritage" to the "healthy building", that the Calouste Gulbenkian Foundation has strategically invested in a gift for the future.

TOUR ITINERARY

Gulbenkian Museum,

Gulbenkian Museum,
entrance

Gulbenkian Museum.
Islamic East

Gulbenkian Museum.
Houdon's Diana

Gulbenkian Museum
seen from the
southern side of the
garden

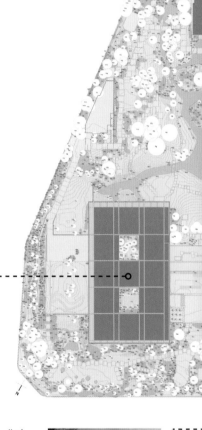

Head-
quarters

Head-
quarters,
entrance
foyer

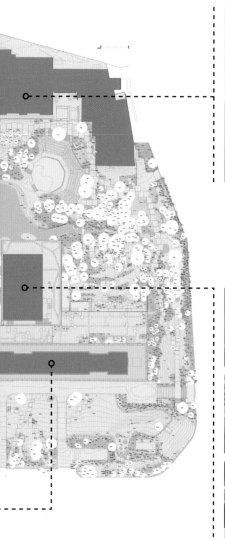

Modern Art Centre.
Main exhibition nave

Modern Art Centre
(CAM) seen from the
north in the garden

Interior of
Auditorium

Aerial view of the
Auditorium

Auditorium Hall.
Access to the
congress area

Auditorium seen
from the garden

Landscape

BRIEF HISTORY OF THE GARDEN

The Calouste Gulbenkian Foundation Garden, which was laid out in the 1960s following a design by the landscape architects António Viana Barreto and Gonçalo Ribeiro Telles, is one of the gardens that most clearly reflect the principles of modern landscape design in Portuguese culture. Those principles are: continuity between the interior and the exterior; functionality; breaking with imposed axialities; the predominance of design of the space over design of forms; the social dimension of the garden; the treatment of ecological and regional matters; respect for the cultural and historical identity of the place; and an apologia of the intrinsic beauty of nature.

Like any other garden, the Gulbenkian garden is an artificial ecosystem placed in a cultural and aesthetic context that offers itself as a space of pleasure, a pleasurable place. To get to know and understand it, one has to experience it in all its plenitude. One has to: delve into all its corners and recesses; interiorise all its sounds; become intoxicated with its balmy air; feel its sweet atmosphere; be seduced by its transitoriness; become disquieted by the quietude that it offers us. The whole garden presents us with space and time to experience the simple things. Of the visitor, the garden merely asks dedication and availability in return.

The peaceful strolls, the calming rest from everyday hustle and bustle, children running and laughing, the beam of light that illuminates the old men's card games, the harmonious singing of the blackcap and the nightingale, the frogs croaking in the twilight, the awkward waddling of the duck with her young, the elegant movements of the capped heron, the smell of morning dew on the grass and of freshly mowed meadow, the balmy vanilla fragrance that rises from the wood, the evasive colours of the undergrowth flowers, the vivid carmine of the azaleas that invades the interior space, the gentle swaying of the meadow in the breeze and the babbling of the stream are the simple, but rare things in this modern life that the Calouste Gulbenkian Foundation Garden offers us.

These things are so simple that we rarely think of them as the realisation of a concept. However, they began as an idea, as a concept, and were built using a number of complex methods and mechanisms that created the conditions so that the garden – this space of simple things – could be.

They are so simple that they make us forget the complex construction that supports them. For example, we forget that, over a large part of its area, the Calouste Gulbenkian Foundation Garden is a hanging garden.

View from the southern part of the Calouste Gulbenkian Foundation garden

"(...) The chosen architectural solution and the location and functioning of the buildings are so intimately linked to the surrounding green space that it is out of the most perfect continuity between interior and exterior spaces, and their balance and harmony, that, ultimately, the overall solution for the whole complex will emerge. What we are doing is more than merely setting a building in a park, or building a garden to serve a building.

Indeed, we have to find a comprehensive relationship between both the elements that make up the whole that is so close that the composition covers the whole area, that the life of the building itself is extended into "open-air parlours" and also from the latter into the interiors.

As constituent elements of that whole, each of them will retain their clearly defined characteristics without becoming mixed up with each other. They will, however, complement each other and prove their value both in terms of aesthetic aspects and in respect to the individual function of each place and the respective environments.

This is the fundamental principle one has aimed for in the proposed solution. Within that orientation, the park's areas of dense vegetation and the clearings, as well as its topography, will create perspectives that will have an intimate relationship with the buildings' volumes and spaces, given that the later were designed in harmony with the park's most prominent elements.

The plan for the design of the park, which is completely modern it terms of the construction methods and materials to be used and in terms of the specific functions given to each zone, shall have a naturalist basis. The architectural plan adopted demands that, the existing vegetation facilitates and the Founder's interest in nature fully justifies it. (...)"

Excerpt from the descriptive memoir to the preliminary design submitted by António Barreto and Gonçalo Ribeiro Telles, December 1961.

By this we mean the garden that was built on the roof of the Great Auditorium, over the dressing rooms, on top of the Temporary Exhibition Gallery and the Congress area, over the tunnel that links the Headquarters Building to the Modern Art Centre and over the Car Park.

This construction work began in June 1963, after a number of studies that had been in development since 1956 had been drawn up. The landscape architects Gonçalo Ribeiro Telles and Azevedo Coutinho were called in to participate in the process in 1958. The former designed the garden for the Foundation's temporary premises, which housed the Projects and Works Department and the Administrative Department. Azevedo Coutinho elaborated the plan for the regeneration of the existing tree coverage, created the gardening service and also the first nurseries, which today are still a part of the garden.

Aerial view of the
Calouste Gulbenkian
Foundation garden.
2006

Aerial view of the
Calouste Gulbenkian
Foundation garden.
2006

Meadow and
main façade of
the Headquarters
building. 2006

Clearing between
the lake and the
Temporary Exhibition
Gallery. 2006

View from the
Amphitheatre to the
Auditorium. 2006

Some of the garden's
residents. 2006

Children enjoying the
garden. 2006

Longitudinal section
of the Headquarters
building and
Auditorium with
underground tunnels
crossing the garden

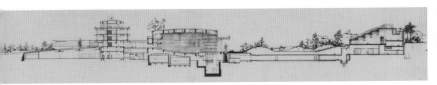

Garden of the
provisional premises

The nursery used in
the first maintenance
work on the garden

Phytosanitary survey
of the vegetation
existing in the park

Commencement
of works with the
containing wall
to preserve the
eucalyptus and the
"kiosk"/belvedere

This concern with conserving the tree coverage and creating the nurseries and gardening service was justified by the importance and significance that Santa Gertrudes Park held for both Azeredo Perdigão and the design team.

Santa Gertrudes Park, which had been purchased by the Vilalva family in the late 19th century, was the ideal place for housing the Calouste Gulbenkian Foundation, not only because of its surface area and location, but also for the fact that it was a park.

Although the park had been home to the Lisbon Zoological Garden (1884-94) and the *Feira Popular* fair (1943-57), its character of landscaped park idealised by Jacob Weiss – a Swiss gardener hired by Eugénio de Almeida in 1866 – was still identifiable when the Calouste Gulbenkian Foundation's Board of Trustees decided to purchase part of the park to fulfil the wish of its founder.

The dense tree coverage of the park had survived until the 1950s, consisting mainly of leafy deciduous and evergreen trees, of which one can highlight several large Eucaliptus globules. A pond and a belvedere close to it known as the *music kiosk* had also survived.

In the competition programme for the Foundation's Headquarters, Museum and Auditorium (1959), the existence of these elements and the fragile garden spatiality that they defined emerged as the guid-

"From that elegant kiosk, (...) from that elegant kiosk where every Sunday and Thursday the marching bands play an always most varied musical repertoire, one enjoys, after climbing the marble steps, a surprising panorama. Perched above the central pond and commanding views over an extensive area in the whole north-south direction to the entrance gate, the music "kiosk" is the veritable place of choice for those who wish to appreciate the delightful whole from the bird's eye view. (...) What beauty in that pond so vast! (...) A veritable lake in its extension!

A veritable mirror with the calmness of its water! (...) On the banks of the pond are grouped, the most varied in form and aspect and the most interesting species from the plant kingdom – including some specimens of the "Gynerium argentum", whose silky pinkish blooms are as soft as the finest ermine (...) In the background... one can see the northern façade of the magnificent palace in which the owners of São Sebastião da Pedreira Park reside. Between the gate to the Park and the small garden of the palace runs the ring road."

Excerpt from
Occidente magazine,
1884.
Xavier da Cunha

Plan of the Lisbon
Zoological Garden

Wood of elm trees at the time of the construction of the garden

Sketch with vegetation scheme

Aerial view of Santa Gertrudes Park with the temporary Foundation premises

ing principle for the exact location of the built complex. The documentation advocated the concentration of the buildings with a view to sparing the tree coverage, which was regarded as a value added of the space. And that is, indeed, what happened.

The buildings were concentrated as much as possible to protect the trees, which, as Azevedo Coutinho had argued, were the basis for the garden idealised by António Barreto and Gonçalo Ribeiro Telles.

The construction work began in June 1963. However, in January 1962, the designers had already signed a request for the purchase of 330 trees and 100 shrubs. The main purpose of this order was to begin, in the coming spring, plantations in the areas not affected by the construction work on the Headquarters and Museum and on the peripheral rim of the garden, which was to isolate and protect the garden from the views and noise from the outside.

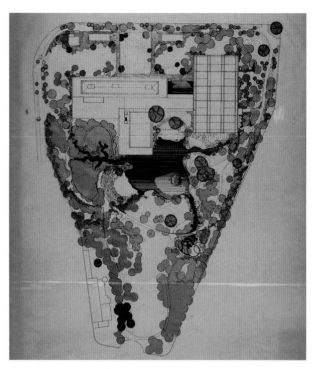

General plan of the Foundation garden design

Under the guidance of the landscape architects, by June 1963 one had defined a number of cautionary measures to be taken into account in the area where the first excavation work was to be carried out. One particular Eucalyptus tree that was considered an outstanding specimen was protected. Trees that were to be used in the design of the future garden were transplanted to the nurseries. And the soil, which Azevedo Coutinho had already upgraded, was removed and deposited in an area that was to undergo interventions at a later stage. In accordance with clause nine of their contract, Gonçalo Ribeiro Telles and António Barreto submitted their final design on 31 March 1963. In August of the same year, work on the garden commenced. It was only concluded in 1969.

Longitudinal section of the garden

Commencement
of work on the
Foundation's
Headquarters and
Museum complex

Commencement
of work on the
Foundation's
Headquarters and
Museum complex

Construction
of the pond

Commencement
of work on the
Foundation's
Headquarters and
Museum complex

Construction of the
underground car park

Construction
of the pond

As far as the garden is concerned, the initial work phase (1965) concentrated above all on the southern zone. The land between the Museum building, pond and the part of the garden to the south of the pond was modelled. The same was done with the land separating the Temporary Exhibition Gallery from the pond.

The area for the open-air Amphitheatre was levelled. The pond was built. Finally, the plantation of the banks of the pond was commenced and the laying of a lawn in the surrounding areas.

In the period from 1966 to 1969, the works concentrated on the expansion of the pond and the whole area to the south of the building complex – following the acquisition by the Foundation of an additional 26-metre-wide slice of Santa Gertrudes Park from Vasco Vilalva – and on the formal definition of the open-air Amphitheatre and the wall enclosing the garden.

Construction of the pond and slab roof of the car park

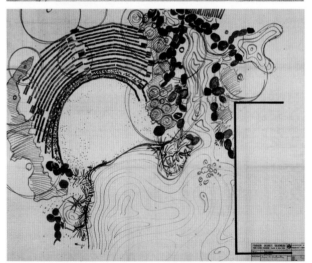

Application of broken stone, gravel and earth on the concrete slab roof of the car park

Design sketch for the Amphitheatre

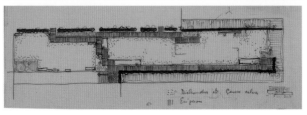

Design sketch for the roofing of the Temporary Exhibition Gallery

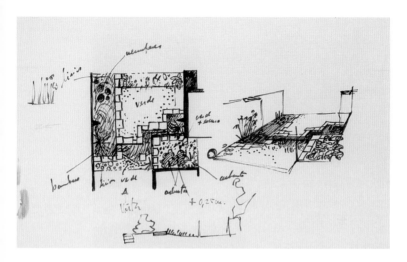

Design sketch for the museum patios

In the same period another phase in the construction of the garden was intensified and work was begun that focused on areas directly related with the buildings, namely: the roofs of Temporary Exhibition Gallery, the Congress area and the Car Park; the patios in the Museum and the Congress area and the flower pots. All the ideas, proposals and solutions for these spaces were developed between December 1961 and March 1963, but the fact that the construction of the building came first had determined that work on them could only begin one year after the commencement of the works.

In mid-1969 the path system – the structure that would reveal the garden to us and would help us to immerse ourselves in it – had not yet been built. It is perhaps better to speak of a walk system, for much more than uniting or crossing different areas of the garden the walks prove to be veritable garden spaces in their own right. It is through them that the character of the garden is best expressed. It is in the walks that the games of light and shade, with their constant element of surprise, that characterise the garden are made most evident. And it is from them that one experiences the spaces of intimacy and sociability and quietude and disquietude that qualify this garden. They are not an opening or a line that cuts its way through the dense vegetation and helps all elements to relate to each other.

They are not the antithesis of garden – they are garden.

Construction of the
Headquarters and
pond

The Museum
and pond under
construction

Construction of the
Auditorium – view to
the garden

Installing the glass
in the window of the
Auditorium

Construction of the
Auditorium and pond

Laying the paths

Aerial view of the
garden with the
construction work
completed

THREE WAYS TO ENJOYMENT

We asked Gonçalo Ribeiro Telles, on the basis of his knowledge and experience of the garden, to define an itinerary or a set of itineraries that would best illustrate all the magic that this space has to offer.

Ribeiro Telles made three suggestions: the light and shade itinerary; the pond itinerary; and the rim itinerary. These three different paths to enjoying the garden refer back to the original themes in the concept developed by the designers when they were invited to design the garden. The descriptive memoir that accompanied the preliminary design in 1961 already stated: "The broad idea based on contrasts of shade and light, tree coverage and glade is the constant aim of the design. Movement, be it in the growth of the plants or in the different aspects of volume, colour and light the plants take on in the different seasons, [...] is also an element to be taken into consideration

General plan, 1969

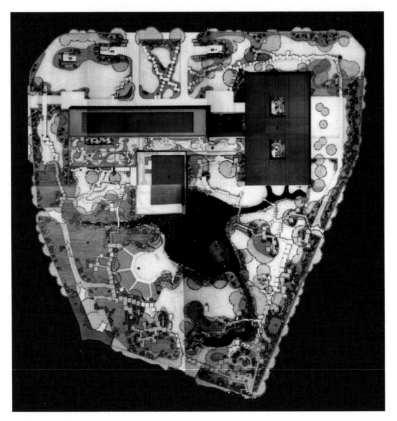

in the development of the project. Likewise, light and how it falls and the projection of shadows and their types [...] are all aspects worthy of study with which one can enrich the whole." If this statement confirms the role of light and vegetation in the design of the garden, then the importance of the role played by water (i.e. the pond) is also expressed in both the care taken in the construction of the pond, the importance it has in the garden and the reflecting capacity of its water.

Hence, in addition to allowing us to experience the garden of today, the itineraries suggested by Ribeiro Telles also propose a journey into the concepts that were at the roots of this space and the history of the whole construction process and the place itself.

To enter a garden is to live a moment, a reencounter of and with the quietude and the disquietude and, as someone has written, to experience the "goodness at the centre of the cyclone". But for that experience to be full and radical we must explore the garden freed from the powers of reason, we must silence and lull our most intimate torments and those of the restless world, we must let ourselves be taken by a state of tranquillity and by the thousand and one sensations that emanate from the garden. In other words, we must be willing to "habitate a pause" and to "be amazed, diffused / trembling in the pure equality of body and space [...]" (Ramos Rosa, *Facilidade do Ar*, p. 55).

View of the garden from the top-floor terrace in the Headquarters building. 2005

1. The light and shade itinerary

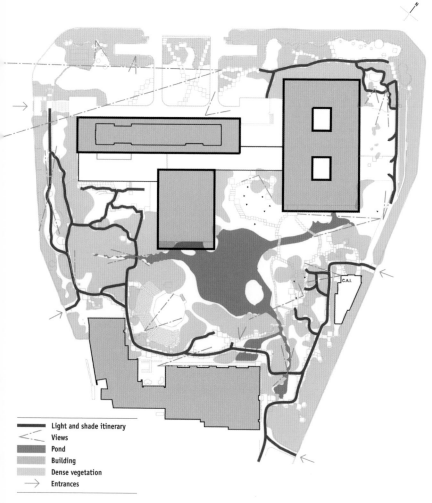

Light and shade itinerary
Views
Pond
Building
Dense vegetation
Entrances

As we walk along the interrupted line to the north of the museum that is defined by the pleasant squares of concrete, Ribeiro Telles affirms: "this garden is a succession of scenarios. There are no points of escape. There are scenarios that succeed each other, constructed by light and shadow". This statement reflects one of the basic concepts that oriented the design of the garden: manipulation of the light.

The light of which we speak is the piercing, brilliant Mediterranean light of Lisbon that hides nothing and exposes all and, for that reason, dissolves any profundity of the space.

The itinerary we are now taking clearly illustrates the game of light/dark generated by the dense groups of vegetation, which, by preventing an immediate and direct reading of the space and its limits, define areas of shade and semi-shade that give the space a profundity that it lacks in reality and that would otherwise not be permitted by the light.

Each step we take, the game of light and dark, of seeing and not seeing, creates a constant effect of surprise, turning the garden into a chain of imagetic moments generated by our progression. This construction gives the space we are walking through a kinetic dimension that motivates us to move, to discover.

View of the garden – glade. 2005

View of the garden – path through trees and shrubs. 2005

View of the garden. 2005

View of the garden. 2005

View of the garden – pond. 2005

This language of the space that negates imposed axialities is a manifestation of the ideals of the modern movement in garden design. Also, the presence of ample lawn areas and simple places of contemplation that manifest concerns with ecological principles and the structure of the landscape mirror those ideas.

The landscape is represented here by the vegetation, to a large extent made up of spontaneous species from Portuguese woods: oak, arbutus, hawthorn, lily-of-the-valley, poplar, ash, lotus, laurel, willow, rushes.

Each species (be it tree, shrub or herbaceous plant) corresponds to a precise ecological reality determined by the morphology of the land: generous oaks occupy the gentle slopes designed in the garden; leafy poplars, ash and alders mark and reinforce the sinuous concavities that run through the garden; proud stone pines and cypresses cover the little hills that break up the space; vivid meadow adorns the clearings that open up in the garden. Each species belongs to Portuguese wild flora or, thanks to the universal character of our culture, to the flora that our cultural development adopted as its own. All of them are in their due place. With them one has created the woods, designed the garden rims and opened up the clearings that evoke the Portuguese landscape.

Let us continue on our walk. The Museum building, on our right, accompanies us with the sobriety of its form and scale, emerging as an integral part of the design of the space. It is not imposing.

Crossing the little mound with yew trees on the right, we enter into the rim of the park – another one of the new gardens that Gonçalo Ribeiro Telles has designed – which protects and isolates the garden from the outside world. The paving in pumice stone, the tropical vegetation and mist produced by the misting system and the tree coverage that envelopes this space create a place with a very expressive ambience in the morning, in the first rays of light of the day.

On the other side, behind a thick curtain of vegetation, is a small pond of water lilies that announces its presence through the intense croaking of the frogs. It is an intimate place worked on a small scale and, perhaps for that reason, it is particularly fascinating for children. Overlooking one of the banks of the pond is a small belvedere that is frequently enveloped by an aroma of curry released by the *Helichrysum stoechas*. At the end of the day in spring and summer, small bats seek this place out to hunt insects.

A grass covered slope leads to a large undulated clearing, which begins next to the east façade of the Museum and Library. It represents, according to Ribeiro Telles, the best concept of a children's park

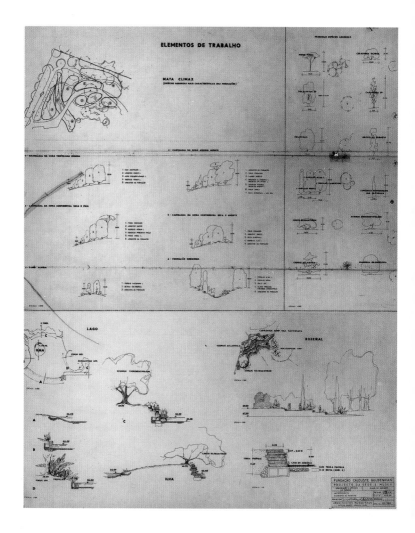

Final design –
vegetation study.
1963

– a space where children can run and play freely and with a certain degree of creativity as they are without the usual plastic and metal equipment that would restrict their fantasy.

Below the concrete balcony on the first floor, on the southern extreme of this façade, a panoramic view opens up that accompanies the line of water and announces the heart of the garden: the great opening of the pond surrounded by a curtain of vegetation, mostly shrubs.

Progressing along the walk we are offered a shady place full of musicality from the water running in one of the babbling streams

View of the garden
– small pond by the
Museum. 2005

View of the garden.
2005

View of the garden
– Museum balcony.
1969

View of the garden
– Museum balcony.
2005

that feed the pond and the quacking of the ducks and sounds of the many other birds that contrasts with the world of light and colour of the glade.

Along the edge of the curtain that conceals and protects the pond, there are moments of reflection, places of intimacy, both formal and informal. It is the world of shadow. Concrete tables and benches forming little retreats invite the visitor to study, have a snack or play cards in the shade of the giant hundred-year-old Eucalyptus trees.

View of the garden.
2005

View of the garden.
2005

View of the garden.
2005

A reminder of times gone by, they are what remains of the trees that came from France in 1866 when Jacob Weiss designed the Santa Gertrudes Park.

The section of this itinerary next to the façade of the José de Azeredo Perdigão Modern Art Centre reveals a different luminosity. The lack of trees, the light reflecting in the water and the white walls give rise to a more luminous spatiality. Very agreeable in the late afternoon, when the shadows have taken over the rest of the garden. This luminosity speaks to us of days gone by when there was a glade here that opened onto the Santa Gertrudes Park, but which had to make way for the Modern Art Centre. The small, recently-planted group of stone pines will soon define a zone of closed shade as opposed to the luminosity that now reigns.

When we speak of light and shade we mean not only the dialogue established between the wood and the glade, but also the light of the glade, which varies according to its location and surroundings, and the filtered light of the wood, which takes on the most diverse expressions depending on the characteristics of each tree that the light passes through.

The western area of the garden – with a dense wood of oak, nettle tree, lily-of-the-valley and Japanese cheesewood, through which a stream flows – is currently one of the most shaded areas of the garden. A place of tranquillity and contemplation, marked by the sound of running water and the chirping of the birds in the trees, this is a space much sought out by young couples.

Study for the southern part of the garden. 2005

View of the garden – pine trees to the south. 2005

View of the garden – rose garden. 2005

Suddenly, the light breaks through the shade. The wood disappears giving way to a clearing with rose beds delimited by the south façade of the Foundation's Headquarters building. It is a space full of light, colour and fragrances.

The intelligent and subtle way in which the building articulates with the garden, from a group of concrete platforms that extend from the different implantation elevations of the building into the garden, is particularly evident in this space. This perfect interaction confers upon the space a hybrid quality, so much so that it can be confused from the inside of the building with an interior patio.

Further to the west next to the itinerary we have been exploring, another place opens up in the interior of the rim. The vapour from the mist systems, a succession of round mirrors of water, the veritable "eyes of the garden", the strong colour of the pumice stone that covers the surface plane, the light at the close of the day, filtered by the dense canopy of the nettle trees create a surprising place. This is a micro-garden made of light, sounds, reverberation. The "garden's eyes", made of black gravel, offer an enigmatic profundity to the plane we walk on by reflecting the sky and the foliage of the trees. This magic place is the perfect terminus to the light and shade itinerary proposed by Ribeiro Telles.

View of the garden – new interventions in the west. 2005

View of the garden – new interventions in the west. 2005

2. The pond itinerary,
or the way to the heart of the garden

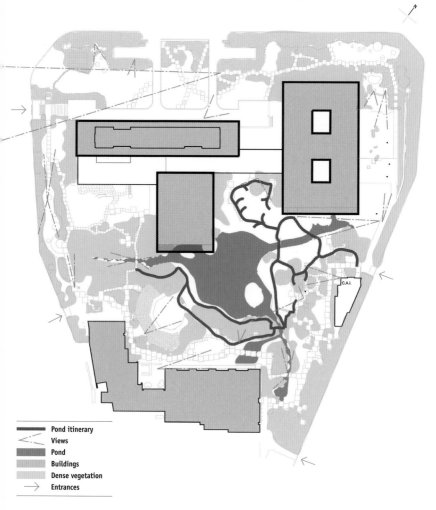

Pond itinerary
Views
Pond
Buildings
Dense vegetation
Entrances

Because the pond and its surroundings are the essence and the heart of the garden, one arrives at it along the route described above, using a series of short, almost secrete trajectories that penetrate a copse of trees and dense shrubbery. The thickness of the vegetation conceals the objective of the routes from our eyes, but we feel that we are approaching a shell. The different types of trees, shrubs and herbaceous plants that surround us, as if in a tunnel, indicate and anticipate the presence of water. Let us enjoy a little longer these shady, secretive and fragrant retreats, where, now and again, the light is caught by the calm surface of the pond.

The intimacy, isolation and contention determined by the scale of the paths we have been walking and the dimension of the vegetation that embraces them are followed by the amplitude, sociability, colour and light that the spacious grassy clearing around the pond offers.

View of the garden. 2005

View of the garden – pond. 2005

View of the garden – pond and Museum. 2005

It is here, in this concave shell defined by the slope we have just been exploring and the south façade of the building that a large number of the garden's visitors choose to gather. Some enjoy observing the garden from the outdoor café next to the building; others rest or play on the grass. We move towards there with the clear feeling that we have reached the essence of the garden, if not what we can call the Time of the Garden.

It is in this place – where three streams converge in the interior of the shell designed and constructed between 1963 and 1966 – that the pond offers itself as an enormous mirror reflecting the light, revealing the great discourse of the water.

It is here, too, that we feel the furthest away from the hustle and bustle of modern life. The naturalist language with which the pond was built, the vegetation that frames it, the image of heaven on earth that the physicity of the water provides, the game of profundities that all these elements determine and the presence of the island enhances, as well as the ecological diversity and richness that this humid system guarantees add to this feeling. The city evaporates. Its noise is softened by the sculpted land and vegetation that configure the garden. The wind blowing from the north becomes a beneficent breeze thanks to the permeable obstacles it encounters on the way. The garden reveals itself in all its plenitude.

The idyllic calm that this space instils in us brings to mind the "Island of Love" evoked by Portugal's greatest poet, Camões, in Book IX of *The Lusiads*: "Where in a smiling vale the mountains end / Form'd in a crystal lake the waters blend / Fring'd was the border with a woodland shade / In ev'ry leaf of various green array'd / Each yellowting'd, each mingling tint between / The dark ash-verdure and the silv'ry green / The trees, now bending forward, slowly shake / Their lofty honours o'er the crystal lake".

View of the garden – opening between the pond and the Temporary Exhibition Gallery. 2005

View of the garden – opening between the pond and the Temporary Exhibition Gallery. 2005

Study for the pond island. 2005

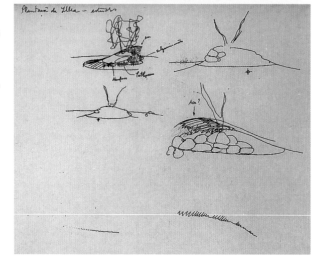

No matter what route we take to approach the lake, we always have to come through the vegetation that first conceals and protects this place and then reveals it in its full glory. One understands this best when the way to the pond takes one through the dense vegetation to the west or the Amphitheatre. Here one can take in the most well known panoramic view of the Gulbenkian Garden: the dialogue between the calm surface of the pond and the building, particularly with the huge window in the south façade of the Auditorium. The grandiose volume in inert concrete of the Auditorium advances towards the pond in an almost perfect syntony between inert and living materials – a duality we often consider to be contradictory.

The mastery with which this area of the garden was designed and built, in accordance with the ecological principles of a functioning landscape, makes us forget that the scenario we witness is an artificial one. We even forget that part of this landscape is a hanging garden built on the dressing rooms and support areas of the Auditorium.

View of the garden – Amphitheatre. 2005

View of the garden – window of the Auditorium looking on the pond. 2005

Plantation study for the banks of the pond. 1963

Study for the pond. 1963

Sketch – pond. 1963

Sketch – pond. 2006

Sketch – pond. 1963

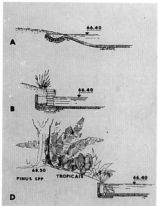

The pond was studied and designed in meticulous detail, always in close interaction with the buildings, in particular the Auditorium, the Amphitheatre and the Temporary Exhibition Gallery, with which it establishes relations of limits, profundity and complicity.

The pond and the covering of the roofs of the car park, the Temporary Exhibition Gallery and the Congress area, which was the result of construction methods that were highly innovative at the time – they were built in concrete with the joints filled with a substance identical to tar that guaranteed the waterproofing, dilatation and contraction of the construction elements – illustrate a high degree of technical knowledge on the part of the landscape architects who designed the garden.

The undulated solution on the non-rocky part of the perimeter of the pond was the means found for concretising the image of a continuous bank that can be found in certain stretches of the pond's perimeter. The thus defined concavity, when filled with top soil, created the conditions for the planting of water-loving plant species and guaranteed continuity between the pond surface and the adjacent spaces.

Along the rest of the pond banks, submersed stone slab walls create a box that allows for plantation. The use of these techniques in both the construction systems conceals the constructed appearance of the banks.

This artificial naturalness of the pond is enhanced by the presence of wild birds, which, immediately after conclusion of the work, colonised the garden both as a nesting and a resting place, adding to the garden with their chirping and warbling and their flights that cut the blue of the sky. The daily variations in the level of the pond water, particularly in the summer months when the water is used for watering the garden, also accentuate the naturalistic character of this completely designed and built landscape.

The pond we can enjoy today is also a reminder of the garden's past. Its inspiration was the original pond designed by Jacob Weiss in 1866, but it by no means mimics its predecessor. Which is only natural. In 1961, the design of the pond resulted from the knowledge the designers had of landscape functioning and construction and the relationship between the pond and the whole. The water surface is always the natural continuity of the various surroundings it comes into contact with and is never an overlapping or a rupture, contrary to the design of the pond in 1866, as the maps of the period show.

The great eucalyptus tree sheltered in a recess of the building is a legacy from this period and has since been classified as an "outstanding tree". Its classification refers to its size, age and history but it was only possible because, in 1958, Azevedo Coutinho, wanted it to be saved and because, during the construction work on the Auditorium, the architects, landscape architects, engineers and gardeners protected it and defined the recess of the building.

Now let us leave the musing and calm that the heart of the garden with its form, matter and spatiality has created in us. Let us seek out other spaces and ambiences, which, together with the light, shade and water, make up the Calouste Gulbenkian Foundation Garden.

View of the garden – glades next to the pond. 2005

View of the garden – eucalyptus tree next to the Auditorium. 2005

3. The rim itinerary

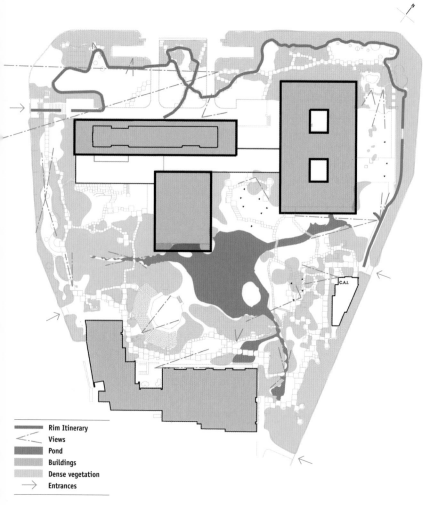

▬▬▬	Rim Itinerary
‹‑‑	Views
▬	Pond
▓	Buildings
░	Dense vegetation
→	Entrances

A feeling of limit, extremity, border is common to the various interpretations of the word rim.

This idea of finiteness in the semantic interpretation of the word rim gains in dimension and importance when one speaks of the rim of a garden. For the epithet of "Eternal Spring" that any garden has, or desires to have, very often finds realisation in nature and in the presence of the defining limit. Indeed, the Indo-European root of the word garden confirms the importance of the limit in defining the spatiality and in the purpose the garden is meant to serve during its existence. The rim of a garden is more than simply a limit or a perimeter that surrounds the garden and is almost external to it. It is much more than that. It is the guarantee of its physical integrity and its spatiality.

Most of the times, if not always, it is with the definition of the limits that the design and construction of a garden begins. It was thus in the Calouste Gulbenkian Foundation Garden. If you were to ask us to pinpoint a date for the beginning of the construction of this garden, the answer would come immediately. Of the various possible dates one could put forward, there is one that imposes itself: January 1962. When António Barreto and Ribeiro Telles ordered 330 trees and 100 shrubs from the Jardim Primavera company for the purpose of beginning the plantation of a full and well-constituted vegetation border, above all in the west, north and east sections, that would protect the garden from external aggressions.

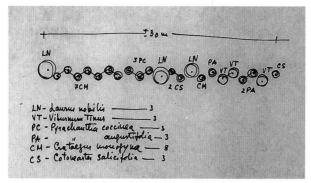

Plantation plan. 1963

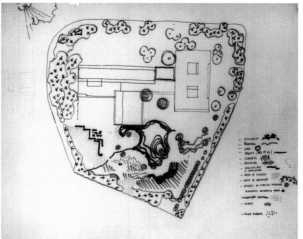

Study for the distribution of vegetation. 1963

Almost fifty years later, that "hedge" has gained in volume, dimension and development thanks to the permanent work of nature on the structure the designers had idealised. This ongoing construction is not a peculiarity of this garden. On the contrary, it is common to all gardens. However, here it emerges with greater expression and greater strength, generating spaces with maturity, temporal density and a greater degree of complexity, heterogeneity and diversity. For Gonçalo Ribeiro Telles, they must be revealed and experienced. They must be opened to the public, for they reveal the construction and spatiality that nature has created over a period of fifty years. This perception is fundamental for creating awareness of the garden as a living, dynamic and, consequently, mutating system.

Studies for the vegetation management. 2006

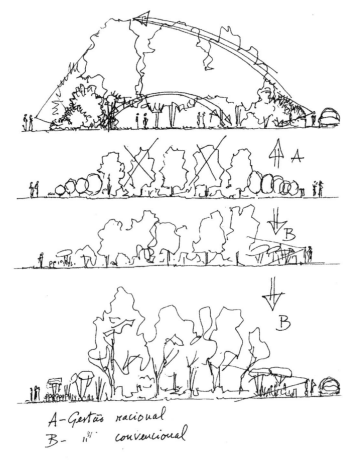

A- Gestão racional
B- " convencional

This itinerary offers all this – the experience of new places of enjoyment. Whereas the two previous itineraries, for the most part, were those defined in the initial design project, this one is completely new and it reveals places and moments that were never experienced before. It is part of the new interventions that began in the year 2000.

Taking this route is revisiting a habitat that is familiar to man, for, as Ribeiro Telles says, "we are an animal on the edge". But it is also experiencing a space of transition between two antagonistic works that complement each other. A line of contact between the wood and the clearing, the rim is a world of contrast – between light and shade, coolness and heat, seeing and being seen, seclusion and sociability – and ecological diversity.

The route stretches from the west entrance to the garden facing the 17th century palace that is the Spanish Embassy, to the gate on the eastern side opening onto Avenida Marquês Sá da Bandeira. The protective rim of the garden is always with us along the way. Here and there, the path makes incursions into the interior, but most of the time we experience the exterior.

Narrow secondary paths, made of small slabs of granite, invite us to immerse ourselves in the outermost zones of the garden. Next to the northern boundary, the rim that has grown freely over the last fifty years has given rise to a small, but in botanical terms very heterogeneous, wood environment. A gently undulating and colourful meadow covers the clearing, which has been on top of the underground car park since 2002. Its floral composition and the different grasses and other herbaceous species that make up the chunks of colour that frame and penetrate the meadow, give the area its seasonal mutations, which, in turn, give us a notion of the passage of time – not only over the duration of one day, but throughout the whole year.

The statue of Calouste Sarkis Gulbenkian by the master sculptor Leopoldo de Almeida, which was transferred to his spot when construction work on the Modern Art Centre commenced, greets those entering the city centre from Praça de Espanha. Photos

The Foundation's Headquarters building features prominently in this stretch of the itinerary, revealing the role of integration of the building into the landscape performed by this part of the garden. It is in the interior of the rim on the northern limit of the garden that we are surprised by little unexpected secluded and intimate retreats.

For some of the way, this discreet, less exposed itinerary designed on the scale of the solitary walker, accompanies, though at a little distance, the light and shade itinerary we have explored above.

View of the garden –
northern zone. 2005

View of the garden –
northern zone. 2005

View of the garden
– statue of Calouste
Gulbenkian. 2005

View of the garden –
meadow. 2005

At times, the paths cross, for, similar to the first itinerary, this one also lives off the complicity between light and shade.

As it adapts to the morphology of the land, and thanks to its intrinsic characteristics, one has a strong feeling as one walks this route of the sculpting of the land that configured this garden. That feeling is particularly strong on the footbridge along the sculpted land on the eastern limit that protects the garden from the bustle of the neighbouring avenue and from possible flooding, to which this part of the city is susceptible. The footbridge brings us to the end of this itinerary, as it takes us away from the rim and into the wood.

View of the garden –
new path. 2005

The purpose of this guide is to give the reader an idea of the distinct spatialities the garden offers. We are fully aware that there is much more to be told, to be described, on the history, life and environment of this space. We have not spoken of the interior patios in the main building, or the garden on the roofs of the Auditorium, the Congress halls and the Temporary Exhibition Gallery. And many other secluded spots and moments and fascinating aspects the garden offers have gone unmentioned.

Museum patios.
2005

Congress zone patios.
2005

But they are there. Waiting to be discovered. To make that discovery and experience fully rewarding one has to use one's senses. For through them we internalise and appropriate the living, pulsing world full of murmurs, fragrances, light and shade that is the garden. And one should never forget that:

– Seeing is offering a multiplicity of images to the purity of the glance; allowing oneself to be taken by the forms, colours, tonalities, shades and lights that make up the garden; seeking out that which conceals itself. Seeing means existing a little all over the place, resting one's glance on the trunk of a tree, abandoning oneself in the still and gleaming mirror of water, reposing in the infinite.

– Listening means hosting the intimacy of the garden, that which is not visible, within us; it is the murmur of the wind, the rustle of the leaves, the babbling of running water, the chirping of birds, the far off noises of the outside world muffled by the vegetation.

– Smelling is transforming the fragrance into cognitive images that evoke memories of other times, other spaces; it is negating our corporeal dimension and that of the garden and is the revelation of the ethereal, of the atmosphere.

– Touching is allowing oneself to be enveloped by the fresh, sweet and crystalline breeze that blows through the garden; it is offering our sensitive bodies to the embracing contact with that other body – living and rich in diversity – that is the garden.

– Tasting is the most intimate bond we can have with the garden; the whole garden is rewritten, is embodied in us when we take pleasure in the sweet, bitter and bittersweet tastes of its fruits, flowers and waters.

PHOTOGRAPHIC SOURCES AND CREDITS

With the exception of those identified below, all photographs were taken from the Calouste Gulbenkian Foundation Archives and created by the authors during all phocers. The drawings were photographed by José Manuel Costa Alves.

Arco do Cego Archives – Lisbon City Council – page 10 b, c

Carlos Ramos Archives – page 14 h

Lisbon Photography Archives – Portuguese Photography Centre – Ministry of Culture – page 11 d

Municipal Photography Archives – Lisbon City Council – page 8 b

José Sarmento de Matos Archives – page 10 a

Keil do Amaral Archives – page 14 g

Marco Albini Archives – page 14 i

Maria Luísa Cid Archives - page 18 c

Teresa Nunes da Ponte Studio – pages 44 b, c, e, f, g

Carlos Azevedo – page 44 a

Private Archives of the Family of the Countess of Vill'Alva – pages 11 b; 57 a, b

Gabinete de Estudos Olisiponenses – Lisbon City Council – pages 10 d; 57 c

The French Government – page 14 k

Jorge Martins Lopes – page 43 d

José Manuel Costa Alves – pages 7; 25 d; 28 a, b, c, d, e, f, g; 30 b; 33 d; 35 e; 38 a, b; 43 a, b, c; 44 d; 46 a, b, c, d, e, f, g; 47 c, d, e, f; 65; 67 a, b, c, d; 70 a, d; 71 b; 72; 73 a, b; 75 b, c; 76 a, b; 77 a, b; 78 b; 79 a, b; 84 a, b, c, d, e; 85 a, b

Mário de Oliveira – pages 11 c; 22 b, c, d, e; 23 d, e, f, g; 25 c, e; 27 c, d, e, f; 29 a, b, c, e; 30 a; 31 a, b, c, d, e , f; 33 a, b; 35 f, g; 36 a; 37 e, f, g; 42 b, c, e; 47 a, b; 58 a, c; 60 a, b, c, d, e, f; 61 a, b; 63 a, b, c, d, e, f, b; 70 c

Marc Treib – pages 67 e; 70 b, e, f, g; 75 a

PH3 – Manuel Silveira Ramos e Jorge Castro – pages 33 d, e, f

Reinaldo Viegas – page 42 a

Arquitectura Magazine – pages 14 c, e; 18 a, c; 36 b

RIBA Library Photographs Collection – page 14 j

Traços na Paisagem – pages 66; 74; 80